Advance Praise for. Locally grown

"This book is for those that congregate in the kitchen. The purpose of this book is the reason I became a chef."

-Lee Richardson, Executive Chef, Capital Hotel, Little Rock, Arkansas

"Who better than Annamary Thompson and Larry Burton to create this collection of creative, intriguing recipes? All were born of their joie de vivre, and their love of the social aspects that surround the preparation of good food made from fresh, locally procured ingredients. They didn't set out to write a book. They set out to live a good life in which food plays a starring role. And their readers now are the beneficiaries."

-Kelley Bass, Restaurant Reviewer for *The Arkansas Times, AY Magazine,* and *Soiree*

"Larry Burton and Annamary Thompson's weekly Hot in Little Rock column "Raise a Glass" always inspires fresh food and wine and reminds us of the joy of cooking with friends and family. We look forward to enjoying the recipes found in these pages."

-Melissa Thoma & Faith Anaya, Uncorked Live!™

Locally Grown:

Recipes Inspired by Local Living

Larry Burton and Annamary Thompson

Temenos Publishing: Little Rock, AR

Cover art by Doug Norton.

ISBN 978-0-9785648-8-9

*T*emenos Publishing
411 Main St.
Argenta Arts District
North Little Rock, AR 72114
501-772-7602
www.temenospublishing.com

Introduction

It really is amazing how some things start to take shape, even before you realize it. This book began life as meals prepared at home for the enjoyment of family and friends. We all enjoy the process of cooking – the enjoyment of opening up a bottle of wine, congregating in the kitchen and preparing a meal.

Sometimes when we entertain, the whole party gets in on the fun – chopping and peeling and washing. And sometimes we won't sit down until 9:00 for dinner. But that's all a part of the process. Eating for us is much more than simply something we have to do to stay alive. Eating for us is an entire experience. It encompasses all the senses and means friends and family are around. We treasure these evenings of cooking – where the process is more the main event than the meal itself.

When I began the five-day-a-week *Hot In Little Rock* lifestyle brand and publication, I asked my father, Larry, to become the food and wine contributor. He eats meat, I do not. Well, I do eat fish.

Then subscribers began to ask me for the recipes. Some couldn't believe we actually live this way. Others received the recipes while in the grocery store, thus solving their dinner quandary. Always looking for more ways to respond to my readership, I thought a *Hot In Little Rock Cookbook* would be just the ticket.

But what sets us apart? What makes us tick? This book went through several different titles, ranging from the straightforward to the silly. I finally took a step back and asked myself, why do people read what we write every day? And the answer became crystal clear. We write about living local. We write about enjoying everything that's special about being right where we are.

There are so many great things to do in Central Arkansas, things the rest of the world hasn't discovered because they haven't bothered to ask. Maybe it took an outsider to see the beauty of this area. I've lived in Massachusetts, Colorado, Illinois and West Virginia. But I've lived in Little Rock now for 15 years. And I'm still amazed at how much there is to do without leaving the comfort of our hometown.

The Farmers' Market in the Argenta area of downtown North Little Rock is certified – meaning they guarantee that all produce and products sold are grown and made in Arkansas. Some other farmers' markets can't say the same thing. We have sustainability networks. We have the world headquarters for Heifer International. We have people working everyday to make sure that what we get right here is the best and freshest and sustains all of us – from the farmer to the consumer.

So the title Locally Grown really says it all. We strive to buy local products where we can. We want the local farmer and craftsman to sustain their business. We are a local business, too. That's what makes America tick – the entrepreneur. And we want to support all of them. When we travel, we still practice living local. Why would we not? It's the best way to experience life.

Of course, part of what we do in our Tuesday edition of *Hot in Little Rock* is to talk about a great wine and pair it with one of our tried and true family recipes. It's hard to pair specific wines in a cookbook, as years change a wine's composition and character. So while there are no actual pairings of food and wine, there are some suggestions that have made sense to us.

We hope you enjoy cooking with us and practicing our motto of living locally.

From our family to yours.

Annamary Thompson
January 2010
www.hotinlittlerock.com

TABLE OF CONTENTS

Soups & Starters

Breads

Main Dishes

Meat Dishes

Fish Dishes

Vegetarian Dishes

Sides

Desserts

About the Authors

SOUPS & STARTERS

Dried Apricot Appetizer

These are wonderful all by themselves, but especially when served with a Vionger or Sauvignon Blanc.

Ingredients

1 package dried apricots

6 oz goat cheese

1/4 cup milk

1 package walnut halves

1/4 cup honey

Instructions

1. If apricots are whole, cut in half.

2. Mix goat cheese with just enough milk to make a smooth mixture.

3. Spoon a bit of goat cheese into the hollow of each apricot.

4. Drizzle two or three drops of honey on the goat cheese.

5. Top with a walnut half.

Mushroom Appetizer

We've been serving these for years. The recipe is easy and the mushrooms will keep in the refrigerator (if there are any left).

Ingredients

1/2 cup wine vinegar

2/3 cup olive oil

1 tsp dried tarragon

1 clove garlic (minced)

1/2 tsp sugar

1/2 tsp salt

1/2 tsp pepper

1 pint box of mushrooms

Instructions

1. Brush any dirt off the mushrooms.

2. In a bowl, whisk all ingredients (except mushrooms) together.

3. Add mushrooms.

4. Cover and refrigerate overnight.

5. To serve, drain mushrooms and place on a plate with a toothpick in each one.

Figs with Prosciutto

Living locally means shopping at the best farmers' market you can in order to get the freshest produce. Fresh figs are available only seasonally, but worth the wait. We serve these with Prosecco.

Ingredients

16 fresh, ripe figs

8 slices of good Prosciutto

1/2 lb Asiago cheese

Toothpicks

Instructions

1. Wash the figs and remove the stems.

2. Slice each fig almost in half.

3. Cut each slice of prosciutto in half, lengthwise.

4. Slice 16 one inch x half inch pieces of cheese.

5. Wrap each fig in prosciutto and secure with a toothpick.

6. Place wrapped figs on a broiler pan and broil for 3-5 minutes, until prosciutto begins to crisp and cheese begins to melt.

Southwest Grits Cakes

These are popular at wine or cocktail parties. They are as easy as they are good. These pair well with a good local beer.

Ingredients

2 cups of quick grits

8 cups of salted, boiling water

2 8-oz packages of Mexican blend shredded cheese

3 4-oz cans of diced green peppers

2 cloves of garlic (finely minced)

1/2 tsp Cayenne pepper

Instructions

1. Stir 2 cups of quick grits into 8 cups of salted boiling water.

2. When grits begin to thicken, add 2 cloves of finely minced garlic.

3. When grits are thickened, remove from heat.

4. Line a 9x13 baking pan with wax or parchment paper.

5. Mix 12 oz diced green chilies and cayenne pepper into the grits.

6. Add 8 oz of shredded Mexican blend cheese

7. Pour into 9x13 baking pan and smooth.

8. Allow grits to set up (usually about an hour)

9. Sprinkle an additional 8 oz of shredded Mexican blend cheese over the top.

10. Place under broiler just until the cheese melts.

11. Cut into 1 inch square pieces.

May be warmed up or served at room temperature.

Apple Stilton Soup

We first had this delicious soup in a restaurant in London. We loved it so much we have tried to duplicate the taste of that evening. We actually like this with a French Pinot Noir.

Ingredients

3 firm apples (Granny Smith, Gala, etc.)

1 onion, thinly sliced

4 cloves of garlic, minced

2 tbs butter

6 sprigs thyme or 1 tsp dried thyme

2 bay leaves

6 cups chicken (or vegetable) stock

1/2 cup Stilton cheese

1/2 cup cream

1 tbs fresh lemon juice

Instructions

1. Peel, core, and chop the apples.

2. Melt the butter in a skillet and add the apples and onion.

3. Just as the apples and onion become tender, add garlic.

4. Transfer to a pot and add the stock, thyme, and bay leaves.

5. Bring to a boil and simmer until mushy.

6. Remove bay leaves.

7. Stir in cheese and cream.

8. Using an immersion blender, puree the mixture (or do it batches in a blender).

9. Add salt and pepper to taste.

10. Add lemon juice (and more Stilton if you like).

Grilled Salmon Spread

We had an extra piece of salmon we had grilled one night and decided it would make a great starter if we fixed it up. So we devised this spread, which is quite good with a chilled Chardonnay.

Ingredients

1 fillet of fresh salmon that has been grilled and chilled.

16 oz cream cheese (softened)

2 tbs capers (drained)

2 shallots (minced)

1/4 cup cream

1/2 tsp salt

Instructions

1. Place softened cream cheese, shallots, salmon, salt and some of the cream into the bowl of a food processor.

2. Process until completely mixed.

3. Remove to a bowl and with a spatula fold in the capers. (If too stiff, add more cream.)

4. Cover and chill for at least an hour.

Appetizer Pizzas with Gruyere and Arugula

Ingredients

1 batch of pizza dough (see p. 75)

1 pint of fresh, assorted mushrooms

1 bag of pre-washed baby arugula

6-8 oz of shredded gruyere

1 lemon, juiced

butter and olive oil

Instructions

1. Stretch (or roll) dough into a large circle, with the dough about ¼ inch thick.

2. Using a biscuit cutter, create as many small, 2-bite size pizza crusts as the dough will allow and place them on a large baking sheet dusted with cornmeal.

3. Sprinkle shredded gruyere cheese on top each of the individual pizzas.

4. Cut mushrooms into equal slices, toss in a bit of olive oil and salt and place on a baking tray. Roast in a hot oven (500 degrees) for 7-10 minutes.

5. Remove from the oven and distribute equally on the pizzas.

6. Bake pizzas at 500 degrees until edges of the pizzas are golden and the cheese is bubbling.

7. Remove from the oven and let rest for a few minutes.

8. Toss 3 cups of fresh arugula and the juice of one lemon, 2 tablespoons of olive oil, salt and pepper. Top each pizza with a bit of the salad and serve.

Watermelon Gazpacho

This is great for a hot summer day. Served in plastic mugs or bowls it is wonderful for a poolside cookout. We like this with a chilled Sauvignon Blanc.

Ingredients

1/2 small watermelon

1 clove garlic

1 jalapeno pepper, seeded

2 limes, juiced

3/4 cup fresh mint leaves

Instructions

1. Scoop out watermelon flesh into blender or food processor.

2. Blend until it becomes a liquid.

3. Add other ingredients one at a time and blend.

4. Add salt to taste.

5. Chill at least an hour before serving.

6. Garnish with a dollop of yogurt and a sprig of fresh mint.

Fresh Parsley Butter

This is such a simple recipe, it seems crazy to put it in the cookbook, but people LOVE it when we make homemade butter. Everyone is so impressed when we say, "Yes! We made that butter from scratch!"

So here's the secret to making butter easily: You need a Kitchen-Aid stand mixer. That's it.

Ingredients

1 pint of whipping cream

½ cup fresh parsley, chopped

salt, to taste

Instructions

Pour your whipping cream into the stand mixer and attach the flat beater. It is important to cover your mixer with Saran Wrap so cream does not go splashing out all over your kitchen! Turn it on medium to high and let it do its thing for about 10 minutes.

But remember to watch it periodically! When the butter solids begin to separate, you're done. Remove the Saran Wrap and remove all the butter solids from the bowl. Squeeze the butter together over the sink or another bowl, releasing any buttermilk that remains. Then place to the side.

Pour out the buttermilk from your bowl. Put this in another dish for safekeeping. Use it in other recipes that call for buttermilk.

Place your butter back in the stand mixer. Put some chopped parsley in the mixer and salt to taste. Mix the butter mixture only until the parsley and salt are incorporated.

Remove the butter from the mixer. You can mold the butter or simply make a ball and place it in a bowl. Serve with fresh, crusty baguette bread (or the popover recipe on page 43).

Mango Salsa

While on vacation in Florida, we found the local fish seller and bought some fresh snapper that was caught that morning. Having nothing in the kitchen besides some mangoes and herbs, we decided we would create a salsa to place on top of the fish. It was delicious! This salsa can be used to top other fishes, or served on its own with salty chips, too. This is another time to find the best local beer.

Ingredients

2 mangoes

1 ripe tomato

2 ounces of fresh cilantro, chopped

salt

lemon juice

Instructions

1. Dice the mangoes and tomatoes and place in a bowl.

2. Mix in the chopped cilantro and add salt and lemon juice to taste.

Mango Guacamole

We love mangoes and avocados. So it seemed only fitting to combine them. Once we tried it, we were hooked. We're asked to bring this dish to every gathering now.

Ingredients

2 ripe avocados

1 ripe mango

1 bunch cilantro

salt

lime juice

Instructions

Halve the avocados and mash them in a bowl. Combine the diced mango, chopped cilantro and the juice of one lime. Add salt to taste. Sea salt works well for this dish.

Serve with some great homemade tortilla chips!

Deviled Eggs

We love deviled eggs. These are one of our favorite things to make for a poolside picnic, or even for the proverbial church potluck. And they always go fast!

Ingredients

6 hard boiled eggs

¼ cup mayonnaise

2 tbs yellow mustard

1 tsp white vinegar

Salt and pepper to taste

Paprika for garnish

Instructions

1. Peel and slice the hard boiled eggs lengthwise.

2. Then remove the yolks and place them in a small bowl.

3. Mash the yolks and add the mayonnaise, mustard, vinegar, salt and pepper.

4. Taste it! Sometimes, I'll add a bit more vinegar – or even some pickle relish to the mixture.

5. Then fill the egg whites with the mixture and garnish with the paprika.

Red Peppers with Cream Cheese

Here's another one of those appetizers that never stays around. We first had them at our next-door neighbor's house and now we make them all the time!

Ingredients

12-15 (or more!) seeded small red peppers from the Olive Bar at the grocery store

1 package of soft cream cheese (or goat cheese for a tangy alternative)

Instructions

1. Take a pepper and stuff it with cream cheese until it is over flowing.

2. Arrange on serving dish.

Told you they were simple! Now, if you want to mix things up, you might substitute the cream cheese for goat cheese. The peppers are very tangy and the cream cheese softens the tang. The goat cheese adds to the tang. So it just depends what kind of mood you're in!

BREADS

Angel Biscuits

We love biscuits and there are none better than these "Angel Biscuits" which we've been making for years and years.

Ingredients

1 package of instant yeast

2 tbs warm water

5 cups flour

1 tsp baking soda

4 tbs sugar

1 tsp salt

1 cup vegetable shortening

2 cups of buttermilk

Instructions

1. Dissolve yeast in warm water.

2. Mix dry ingredients together.

3. Cut in the shortening.

4. Add buttermilk and then the yeast.

5. Knead for about a minute.

6. Roll out and cut with a biscuit cutter.

7. Bake at 400 degrees for 12-15 minutes.

This dough will actually keep in the refrigerator for up to a week.

For variety you may want to add crumbled bacon or cheddar cheese, or chives, or all three!

Papa's Sweet Rolls

The mini-staffers are always asking for Papa's Sweet Rolls, and after you taste them you will know why. The recipe is one "Papa" grew up with. These also make great dinner rolls.

Ingredients

3 tbs butter or margarine (melted)

½ cup sugar

1 tsp salt

1 package instant yeast

2 cups very warm water

1 egg, beaten

5 ½ cups of flour

1 tsp baking powder

Icing

1 cup powdered sugar

1 tbs melted butter

½ tsp vanilla

A few drops of milk or cream

Instructions

1. Combine the first 5 ingredients in a large mixing bowl.

2. Add 3 cups of flour and the baking powder and mix.

3. Add remaining flour and mix until smooth.

4. Cover and allow to rise.

5. Punch down and roll out into a rectangle.

6. Spread with 2 tbs of melted butter, sprinkle with cinnamon and sugar.

7. Beginning on the long side, roll the dough into a long rope.

8. Cut in the middle, then the middle of each half. Continue until you have the number of large or small rolls.

9. Place in a greased 9x13 baking pan and allow to rise until doubled in size.

10. Bake at 400 degrees for about 10-15 minutes.

11. Ice with a powdered sugar icing.

12. Serve warm (but these are also pretty good cold the next day if there are any left).

For dinner rolls, roll out the dough into a large circle. Using a pizza cutter, slice the dough into wedges. Roll each wedge from the big end to the small, making a crescent. Place on a greased cookie sheet and allow to rise until doubled in size. Bake at 400 degrees for 10-15 minutes.

Mark Bittman's Parmesan Cream Crackers

(Mark Bittman writes a weekly column in *The New York Times*.)

Ingredients

1 cup all-purpose flour

1/2 tsp salt

1/2 cup finely grated fresh Parmesan cheese

4 tbs unsalted butter

1/4 cup cream

coarse salt for sprinkling

Instructions

1. Heat oven to 400 degrees.

2. Line cookie sheet with parchment paper.

3. Place flour, salt, cheese and butter in food processor.

4. Pulse until combined.

5. Add cream and pulse (add more cream if necessary) until mixture holds together but is not sticky.

6. Roll out dough on floured surface until about 1/4 inch thick.

7. Move to cookie sheet.

8. Using a pizza cutter, score the dough into squares.

9. Sprinkle with salt and bake until lightly browned (about 10 minutes).

Mom's Popovers

My mother makes the best popovers – bar none. They are better than the popovers at some of the fancy department store restaurants. If there are special requests to be made, mine is always popovers! These are moist and gooey and best served hot.

Ingredients

1 cup flour

1 cup milk

2 eggs

1 tbs butter

Salt to taste

Instructions

1. Combine all ingredients in a bowl. If the mixture seems too thick, add a bit more milk.

2. Pour into greased muffin tins and bake for 30-40 minutes in a 400 degree oven. They are done when they have "popped" and are brown on top.

3. Turn off the oven and let them crisp for about 5 minutes.

MAIN
DISHES

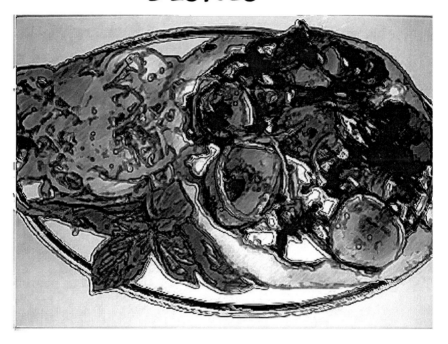

MEAT DISHES
Lemon Chicken with Capers

Serve this with a Pinot Gris or Sauvignon Blanc and you have a great pairing!

Ingredients

4 boneless chicken breasts

1 egg (beaten)

1/2 cup seasoned flour (1 tsp granulated garlic, salt, 1/4 cup grated Parmigiano Reggiano)

3 lemons

2 cloves of garlic

4 tbs olive oil

1 cup white wine

1 6 oz bottle of capers (drained)

additional 1/4 cup of Parmigiano Reggiano

Instructions

1. Zest then squeeze lemons.

2. Wash chicken breasts, pat dry.

3. Dip chicken breasts (one at a time) into seasoned flour, then into beaten eggs, then into flour.

4. Heat a large skillet on medium high and add olive oil.

5. When oil is hot, add chicken breasts.

6. Cook just until the chicken gains some color.

7. Add white wine and juice of two lemons.

8. Cover and simmer until chicken is tender, or about 30 minutes.

9. Remove chicken to a serving plate and cover.

10. Turn up the heat under the skillet and add the zest of two lemons and the juice of one. Reduce slightly.

11. Add capers and pour mixture over chicken.

12. Dust with the remaining Parmigiano Reggiano.

Chicken and Mushrooms in Sherry Sauce

This makes a good buffet main course. We like to serve it with wild rice. A White Bordeaux makes a great accompaniment.

Ingredients

6 boneless, skinless chicken breasts

1 quart of sour cream (low fat is fine)

1 lemon, juiced

1 clove of finely minced garlic

1/2 cup dry Sherry

1/2 cup chicken stock

1 pint fresh mushrooms

4 tbs butter

Instructions

1. Cut the chicken into large pieces about 1/2 inch square.

2. Combine sour cream, lemon juice, garlic and sherry and chicken stock. Mix thoroughly.

3. Quarter mushrooms and sauté in 2 tbs of butter until browned.

4. Place chicken and mushrooms in 9x11 baking dish and pour over the sour cream mixture.

5. Drizzle 2 tbs melted butter over the top.

6. Bake at 350 degrees for approximately 45 minutes.

Mussel and Fennel Salad

This is a great main dish for a luncheon. It takes next to no time to prepare and is sure to win raves from your guests. We, who like wine with lunch and dinner (sticking to coffee and juice for breakfast), like a nice Chardonnay or Sauvignon Blanc with this.

Ingredients

3 lbs fresh mussels

1 cup dry, white wine

2 shallots, minced

1 lemon, juiced

3 fennel bulbs

2 fresh, ripe tomatoes

6 tbs olive oil

2 tbs. minced fresh parsley

Salt and pepper to taste

Instructions

1. Scrub mussels and rinse several times under cold water. Trim the "beards," and place in a large pot and add the wine, shallots, and lemon juice.

2. Bring to a boil, cover and cook until the mussels have opened (about 5 minutes).

3. Remove the mussels and reserve the liquid.

4. Shell the mussels (no need for the shells any more) and set them aside.

5. Strain the cooking liquid (cheesecloth is preferred here).

6. Trim the fennel, slice into rings, discarding the core.

7. Slice the tomatoes.

8. Whisk olive oil with 1-2 tbs of reserved cooking liquid, add parsley, and season with salt and pepper.

9. Arrange tomatoes around one side of a plate, and the fennel around the other.

10. Place the mussels in the middle, and dress with Vinaigrette. Add crusty bread and more wine. Voila!

Jambalaya

When Fat Tuesday approaches, we begin to think of Jambalaya. We enjoy celebrating with masks, beads, good friends, and good food. We've been using this recipe for more than 15 years, and think it works just great. Salad, crusty bread, and a good red wine make this a real celebration.

Ingredients

½ lb hot sausage (remove casings if it comes in links)

1 lb Andouille sausage, sliced

1 large onion, chopped

1 green bell pepper, chopped

2 stalks celery, chopped

8 cloves garlic, minced

1 16-oz can of tomatoes, crushed

1-2 cups chicken stock

2 cups smoked ham, diced

1 lb boneless, skinless chicken breasts, cubed

½ tsp Thyme

3 Bay leaves

Hot Sauce to taste

2 cups rice, cooked

Instructions

1. Sauté hot sausage (use a bit of oil if necessary).

2. Add onions, bell pepper, and celery. Cook until tender.

3. Add bay leaf and thyme, tomatoes, chicken stock, garlic, Andouille, chicken, and ham. Cover and simmer for at least 30 minutes.

4. Meanwhile prepare the rice.

5. When the Jambalaya is ready, put rice in bowls, ladle in the Jambalaya. Sprinkle with chopped green onions and fresh parsley. Serve with bread and a green salad.

Pork Tenderloin with Apples and Calvados Cream

This will make six to eight servings. Spazzle or roasted red potatoes make a good partner. A buttery Chardonnay, Vionger, or Pinot Noir go well with this dish.

Ingredients

2 pork tenderloins

2 cups apple cider

2 tbs butter

3 red delicious apples

1 medium onion

1/2 cup Calvados

1 tsp apple cider vinegar

1 cup half and half

Instructions

1. Place tenderloins in a plastic bag and add 1 cup of the cider. Marinate for a couple of hours.

2. Peel, core and slice apples. Sprinkle with lemon juice.

3. Chop the onion into a fine dice.

4. Place tenderloins on a roasting rack, and bake at 375 degrees for approximately 45 minutes, or until a thermometer registers 160 degrees.

5. Remove tenderloins to a plate and cover.

6. Add 1 cup of cider, 1 tsp cider vinegar, and 2 tbs butter to roasting pan. Mix with drippings over medium heat.

7. Add onions and apples and sauté until tender.

8. Remove onions and apples, and add Calvados.

9. Add cream and heat for about one minute.

10. Slice tenderloin into medallions, put onions and apples on top, and cover with Calvados cream.

Pork Tenderloin with Apricots

Ingredients

1 pork tenderloin (approx 1 ½ lbs)

10-12 dried apricots

1 cup apricot preserves

1 tbs fresh rosemary (finely chopped)

1 tbs mustard

1 clove garlic (mashed)

¼ cup Cognac

Instructions

1. Rub the tenderloins with olive oil, then sprinkle with salt and pepper and a bit of granulated garlic.

2. Pat the rosemary all over the tenderloin.

3. Place on a roasting rack and roast for about 30 minutes at 375 degrees, or until the thermometer registers about 160 degrees.

4. Meanwhile, cut 10-12 dried apricots in half and soak them in very hot water until they are tender.

5. Then combine apricot preserves, Cognac, mustard, and garlic.

6. Add the apricots and heat through.

7. When the tenderloin is done, remove from the oven and wrap in foil to rest for at least five minutes.

8. Then slice, drizzle with the sauce, and serve over a bed of mashed sweet potatoes.

Beef Stew

Especially good on a cold winter night, beef stew needs only a salad and a good red table wine to make this a perfect meal.

Ingredients

2 lbs of boneless chuck or stew meat

2 cloves of garlic

½ cup of seasoned flour

2 cups of beef stock

2 bay leaves

Worcestershire sauce

1 package of frozen pearl onions

2 large potatoes

2 large carrots

15-20 mushrooms

2 stalks celery

Pinch of ground cloves

1 cup red wine

Instructions

1. Cut the meat into 1 inch square pieces.

2. Place the beef into a plastic bag into which ½ cup of flour, salt and pepper has been mixed.

3. Shake it vigorously so all the beef is well coated.

4. Take a good cast iron Dutch oven and heat a few tablespoons of olive oil plus a tablespoon of butter and brown the meat.

5. Then add two cloves of garlic that have been diced.

6. When the garlic is just beginning to turn golden, add 2 cups of beef stock, two bay leaves, and two dashes of Worcestershire sauce.

7. Put the lid on the pan and place in a 350 degree oven for 1 ½ to 2 hours.

8. Remove from the oven, and add the following: 1 package of frozen pearl onions, two large potatoes that have been cubed, two large carrots that have been sliced into coins, 15 (or so) mushrooms, and two stalks of celery that has been sliced into small pieces.

9. Add ¼ tsp of cloves, and a cup of red wine, replace the lid, and return to the oven for 45 minutes.

Chili with Chocolate

We have a friend whose chili has a secret ingredient: chocolate. It gives the dish a wonderfully deep flavor, along with the heat from chipotle peppers. While you may prefer beer with this, we like a good, robust Chianti.

Ingredients

3 large onions, chopped

2 large red peppers, chopped

2 cloves garlic, minced

1 ½ lbs chuck, cut into small cubes

3 tbs brown sugar

2 tbs ancho chili powder

1 tbs unsweetened cocoa

1 tsp ground cumin

½ tsp black pepper

¼ tsp salt

2 cans pinto beans, rinsed and drained

2 cans diced tomatoes, juice and all

1 can fat-free, low sodium chicken broth

2 chipotle chilies (canned in adobo sauce) minced

2 oz unsweetened chocolate, chopped

Instructions

1. Pour 3-4 tbs of good olive oil into a large skillet, and add the diced onion, red bell pepper, minced garlic and the cubed chuck.

2. When the meat is browned and the onion, peppers, and garlic are tender, add the brown sugar, ancho chili powder, unsweetened cocoa, ground cumin, pepper, and salt, pinto beans, diced tomatoes, chicken broth, and chipotle chiles.

3. Cook for at least 30 minutes or until meat is tender. When ready to serve add 2 ounces unsweetened chocolate.

4. When the chocolate is melted and blended into the chili, spoon into bowls and top with sour cream and chopped green onions.

Larry's Cassoulet

We love Cassoulet, but since we usually don't have access to a confit of duck, we have altered the recipe a bit. Choose your wine (red or white) but we prefer a hearty red with this hearty dish.

Ingredients

1 lb sweet Italian sausage (cut into inch long pieces)

1 lb beef chuck (cut into 1 inch cubes)

1 large onion, sliced

2 medium garlic cloves, minced

2 green peppers, seeded and cut into strips

1 lb white beans, cooked

1 tsp basil

½ tsp salt

1 tsp paprika

½ tsp pepper

1 cup strong beef stock

Instructions

1. Brown sausage and place in a 3 quart casserole.

2. Drain the fat but reserve 2 tbs.

3. Brown beef in 1 tbs of the reserved fat and add to casserole.

4. Sauté onion and garlic in remaining fat until tender.

5. Add green peppers and cook for one or two minutes more.

6. Add this to the casserole along with the beans.

7. Sprinkle with the seasonings and toss.

8. Add stock and bake in a 350 degree oven for an hour and fifteen minutes (or slightly longer depending on the beef).

Serve with a green salad.

FISH DISHES

Tilapia with Peppers and Onions

For a quick supper this is a great dish. Pair with your favorite white wine.

Ingredients

4 Tilapia filets

3 Peppers (1 green, 1 red, 1 yellow)

1 medium onion

Milk and flour for coating fish

Olive oil

Instructions

1. Remove the stem and seeds from the peppers.

2. Slice peppers into long strips.

3. Peel onion and slice into thin rounds.

4. Heat 2-3 tbs olive oil in a pan.

5. Sauté peppers and onions just until they are soft. Remove from heat.

6. Dip each fillet in seasoned (salt, granulated garlic, pepper) flour. Then dip into milk, then into the flour again.

7. Heat 3-4 tbs olive oil in a large frying pan.

8. When oil "spits" at you when a bit of water is dropped in it, place fillets into the pan.

9. Cook about 3 minutes per side or until golden.

10.Remove from pan to paper towel then to a serving plate.

11.Place 1/4th of pepper and onion mixture on top of the fish.

12.Serve with a green vegetable and a salad.

Scallops and Crab in Cognac Cream

Seafood lovers usually go back for seconds when we serve this rich dish containing scallops and crab. We think this goes well with a chilled Sauvignon Blanc.

Ingredients

2 lbs sea scallops cut in half

1 large container of fresh, lump crab

1 cup half and half

16 oz of low fat sour cream

8 oz fresh mushrooms

2 large shallots, diced

2 cloves of garlic, diced

3 tbs flour

1/2 cup (or more depending on taste) Cognac

1 lb wide noodles, cooked

½ cup parmesan cheese

1 cup bread crumbs

3 tbs butter

½ cup fresh, chopped parsley

Instructions

1. Sauté mushrooms in 1 tbs olive oil and 1 tbs butter.

2. Add shallots, and finally garlic.

3. Sprinkle with flour and cook for at least 30 seconds.

4. Add half and half and stir until the mixture begins to thicken.

5. Add sour cream, and finally the Cognac.

6. When the mixture is creamy, add the scallops and crab, stirring gently.

7. Put noodles into a greased 9x13 baking dish and add the seafood mixture.

8. Top with a mixture of bread crumbs, parmesan cheese, and 2 tbs butter.

9. Bake for 30 minutes.

10. Sprinkle fresh, chopped parsley over the top.

Sea Bass with Sautéed Spinach

Guests rave over this simple preparation, which we like to serve with sautéed spinach. Depending on your taste, anything from a Fume Blanc to a Veltliner goes well with this.

Ingredients

4 6-oz pieces of fresh Sea Bass

1 cup white wine

1 bunch of green onions

1 large red pepper, julienned

salt and pepper

1 lb fresh spinach (or more!)

1/4 cup toasted pine nuts

2 tbs butter

1 tbs olive oil

1 clove of garlic finely minced

Instructions

1. Cut four 12 inch square pieces of aluminum foil.

2. Place a piece of Sea Bass on each square.

3. Splash with dry white wine.

4. Cut onions into long, thin slices and place a few on the Sea Bass.

5. Arrange a few julienned slices of red pepper on top of the onions.

6. Sprinkle with salt and pepper.

7. Seal packets and place on a baking tray.

8. Bake for approximately 15 minutes at 375 degrees.

9. Meanwhile, wash and remove stems from the spinach.

10. Melt butter and olive oil in a large skillet and sauté the spinach, adding the garlic at the end (to prevent burning it).

11. Add the toasted pine nuts to the spinach and serve along side the Sea Bass.

Clam Linguine

My husband learned to make this dish 20 years ago. Since then, he has been perfecting it. It's a wonderful and light dish that goes well with a chilled Chablis.

Ingredients

Serves 4

8 bunches of green onions – finely chopped

1 bunch of fresh parsley

4 tbs minced garlic

2 cups minced clams with juice

½ cup white wine

Olive oil

Salt and pepper to taste

1 tsp garlic powder

Parmesan cheese for garnish

Instructions

1. Put a small amount of olive oil in a pan over high heat.

2. Sauté the chopped green onions until they become semi-translucent.

3. Add about a cup of finely chopped parsley.

4. When the onions are translucent and the liquid is mostly evaporated, add the wine and combine.

5. Stir until the ingredients begin to congeal.

6. Add the garlic and combine.

7. Continuing stirring until the sauce becomes thick, and then add the clam juice.

8. Continue stirring for 5 minutes.

9. Add salt, pepper, garlic powder and a pinch more of the parsley and clams.

10. Serve over linguine and garnish with parmesan cheese.

Tuna Over Cabbage

This is another one of those great dishes that my husband created during his years of bachelorhood. It's simple and delicious. Pair it with a Sancerre and you're all set for a fabulous dinner.

Ingredients

1 head of cabbage

2 sushi grade tuna steaks

½ cup soy sauce

½ cup honey

½ cup balsamic vinegar

1 tbs pepper

1 tbs sea salt

1 tbs garlic powder

1 tbs grated ginger

½ cup olive oil

Instructions

1. Combine half of the soy sauce, honey and vinegar into a small bowl.

2. Place the tuna steaks in the bowl and marinate for 30 minutes.

3. While the tuna is marinating, chop the cabbage finely.

4. Once the tuna is finished marinating, coat it with the pepper, sea salt and garlic powder.

5. Sear the tuna in olive oil over high heat until black on each side. (About 2-3 minutes per side) The fish will still be raw in the middle.

6. Remove from heat and let sit for 5 minutes.

7. To make the sauce, whisk together the remaining honey, soy sauce, vinegar and ginger with ¼ cup olive oil.

8. Arrange the cabbage on a plate. Place slices of the tuna on top of the cabbage and drizzle the sauce over the fish.

VEGETARIAN DISHES

Pizza with Goat Cheese and Fresh Figs

We have a tradition of pizza on Sunday nights. This pizza goes well with a Pinot Noir.

Ingredients

Dough	Topping
3 cups flour	12-15 fresh, ripe figs
1 tb instant yeast	1 medium, red onion
1 tb sugar	6 oz goat cheese
1 tsp salt	1/2 cup balsamic vinegar
1 cup plus 2 tbs very warm water	

Instructions

1. Place all dry ingredients into the bowl of a mixer equipped with a dough hook.

2. Add very warm water and mix until it makes a ball.

3. Continue kneading for about 4 minutes.

4. Let rise until doubled in volume then knead into a ball.

5. Let the dough rest for a few minutes then place on clean surface dusted with cornmeal.

6. Roll or stretch out into a shape to fit your preferred pan(s) which you have dusted with cornmeal.

7. Crumble goat cheese and scatter over the top of the dough.

8. Slice figs in half and arrange over goat cheese.

9. Slice the red onion into thin rounds, separate and scatter over figs.

10. Bake at 450 degrees until crust is golden.

Separately, place 1/2 cup of balsamic vinegar into a small pan and place over medium heat. Bring to a low boil and reduce by half. Let cool slightly before drizzling over pizza before serving.

Southwest Casserole

When our children were young they each, separately, became vegetarians. So, with two vegetarians in the house, we quickly learned to make some quick, veggie meals. This was always a hit.

Ingredients

1 can chili beans

1 can red kidney beans

1 can corn (not creamed)

1 onion diced

1 green pepper, chopped

1 can diced tomatoes

1 package shredded cheddar cheese

1 box of cornbread mix

Instructions

1. Sauté onions and peppers in olive oil and add tomatoes.

2. Drain the beans and corn and place in a greased casserole dish.

3. Add the tomatoes, onions and peppers.

4. Sprinkle on the cheddar cheese.

5. Prepare the cornbread mix as directed on the package and pour over the top.

6. Bake at 400 degrees until the cornbread topping is golden.

With a green salad, this makes a great, fast family supper.

Oriccetti with Tomatoes, Garlic, and Basil

This dish is as good in the winter as in the summer. Oriccetti is an "ear shaped" pasta. If you can't find it, just use something else! Cut the ingredients in half if you want to serve it as a side dish. We prefer a good Italian red such as Valpolicella Classico.

Ingredients

1 box oriccetti

2 pints of grape tomatoes

1 large bunch of fresh basil

4 cloves of garlic

1/3 cup of good olive oil

1/2 cup of Parmigiano Reggiano

Instructions

1. Cut grape tomatoes in half and place in a large, ceramic bowl.

2. Finely dice the garlic and add it to the tomatoes.

3. Pour the olive oil over the tomatoes and garlic.

4. Add a tsp of salt.

5. In a large pot, bring salted water to a boil.

6. Add the oriccetti and cook until just tender.

7. Drain the oriccetti and transfer to bowl containing the tomatoes, garlic, and oil.

8. Tear the basil into medium pieces and add to the bowl.

9. Add 1/2 cup Parmigiano Reggiano and toss.

Chile Relleno Casserole

We love this on a cold winter evening, but it is actually wonderful in any season. We prefer a spicy Zinfandel with this. We also use fresh roasted chiles from the Farmer's Market when we can get them.

Ingredients

4 7oz cans of whole, mild green chiles

1 pound Monterey Jack cheese

5 eggs

1 1/4 cups milk

1/4 cup flour

1/2 tsp salt

1/4 tsp pepper

4 cups (1 pound) grated mild cheddar cheese

Instructions

1. Slit chiles along one side and remove the seeds.

2. Slice Monterey Jack cheese into 1/4 inch thick slices and place inside the chiles.

3. Lay the stuffed chiles in an ungreased, 9x11 baking dish.

4. Mix eggs, milk, flour, salt and pepper, and pour over chiles.

5. Sprinkle the grated Cheddar over the top.

6. Bake uncovered in a 350 degree oven for 45 minutes.

Greg's Red Sauce

This is enough sauce for about 4 people. It's really a labor of love, but so worth it in the end! This sauce can be served over plain pasta, or mix it up with beef or shrimp. Of course, serve it with a great Pinot Noir.

Ingredients

10 heirloom or roma tomatoes – the fresher the better - chopped

1 large sweet onion - diced

4 tbs garlic

2 tbs parsley

2 tbs oregano

2 tbs basil

½ cup red wine

Olive oil

Instructions

1. Sauté finely diced onion in olive oil until the onion is translucent.

2. Add finely chopped parsley and combine.

3. Add diced tomatoes, chopped basil and oregano.

4. Stir until the sauce thickens.

5. Add the wine and keep stirring.

6. Add garlic, salt and pepper to taste.

7. Cook (keep stirring!) until all the ingredients are incorporated. This takes about an hour.

8. Add a pinch of oregano and basil at the end.

Eggplant Parmigian

This is a great comfort food. I learned how to make this from my mother growing up. In a recent conversation, it turns out that this is really my grandmother's recipe. We had some delicious fried eggplant at a restaurant in New Orleans, but we both agreed that Grandma's wins every time!

Ingredients

1 large eggplant

2 eggs

1 package of saltine crackers

olive oil

2-3 cups of Greg's Red Sauce (Page 83)

mozzarella cheese

Instructions

1. Thinly slice the eggplant and put aside in salt water.

2. Beat the eggs in one bowl and crush the bag of saltine crackers in another.

3. While doing this, put about 1/2 cup of olive oil in a hot pan.

4. Dip the eggplant in the beaten eggs, then coat with the crushed saltines.

5. When the oil is hot, place the eggplant in the pan.

6. Continue doing this until the pan is full of eggplant.

7. Turn the eggplant when it is brown on one side.

8. When the eggplant is brown on both sides, place on a plate to drain.

9. Continue to cook the eggplant and add oil as needed. (It does tend to soak it up!)

Now, you could stop here and just serve as an appetizer. But if you want the full meal, continue on:

10. Arrange the eggplant in an oven safe dish, covering each layer with Greg's Red Sauce.

11. Top with mozzarella cheese and bake at 375 degrees until the cheese is bubbling.

Goat Cheese Salad with Sage Dressing

It was in Prague that we first had this salad and loved it. We've had it several times since and enjoy it more each time. A nice variation is to candy the walnuts. This goes very nicely with a good Chardonnay.

Ingredients

16 oz goat cheese

2 egg whites

1 1/2 cups bread crumbs

2 tbs butter

2 tbs corn oil

2 packages of pre-washed mixed baby greens

1 cup walnut halves

Dressing

1/4 cup cider vinegar

1 cup olive oil

1 tsp sugar

1 tsp dry, rubbed sage

1/2 tsp salt

Instructions

1. Cut goat cheese into 3/4 inch rounds using dental floss (really!)

2. Dip each round into the egg whites and then into the bread crumbs.

3. Refrigerate cheese rounds for at least 30 minutes.

4. Combine ingredients for the dressing and whisk together. Dressing should be just slightly sweet.

5. Heat butter and oil in a heavy skillet.

6. Saute rounds for about a minute on each side, or until they are golden.

7. Dress greens, add walnuts, and place a mound on each plate.

8. Top with 2 or 3 rounds of warm goat cheese.

SIDE DISHES

Grandma's Corn Pudding

We grew up eating this corn pudding/soufflé every time there was a company meal. We still like it!

Ingredients

1 can creamed corn (in season, this is wonderful with fresh corn that has been creamed)

½ cup milk

3 tbs corn starch

½ cup grated cheddar cheese

3 eggs separated

1 tsp salt

¼ tsp pepper

8 saltine crackers, crushed

1 tbs butter

Instructions

1. Pour creamed corn into a soufflé dish.

2. Mix the cornstarch and milk together and add to the corn.

3. Beat the egg yolks and add to the dish, along with the cheese.

4. Add the salt and pepper. Mix well.

5. Now, beat the egg whites until stiff, and fold them into the corn mixture.

6. Top with crushed crackers and dot with butter.

7. Bake in a 350 degree oven for 45 minutes.

Green Bean Bundles

The bundles combine the flavor of the green beans with the mild saltiness of the prosciutto. They make practically any plate look special.

Ingredients

1 1/2 lbs fresh green beans (if you can't find them, use frozen)

4 slices of prosciutto

1 tbs butter

salt to taste

Instructions

1. Wash and remove stems from the green beans.

2. Steam the green beans until they are tender, but still bright green.

3. Cut the prosciutto slices in half, lengthwise.

4. Drain green beans and toss in salt (to taste) and butter.

5. Separate into 8 separate servings.

6. Gather each separate serving into a bundle and wrap in one half slice of prosciutto.

Shaved Fennel Slaw

Fennel has a unique flavor, and when served as a side with broiled or grilled fish, brings great zing to the meal.

Ingredients

1 large or 3 small bulbs of fennel

1 medium red onion

2 large oranges

4 tbs olive oil

2 tbs cider or red wine vinegar

1 tsp sugar

1 tsp salt

1/2 tsp pepper

1/4 cup of finely chopped fennel fronds

Instructions

1. Wash fennel and cut off bottom and fronds.

2. Shave fennel bulb(s) using a mandolin.

3. Peel the red onion and shave it using the mandolin.

4. Peel two large oranges and slice into think rounds.

5. Combine fennel, onion, and oranges in a large bowl.

6. Combine all remaining ingredients in a small bowl and whisk.

7. Pour over the slaw and chill.

Sautéed Carrots, Eggplant and Mushrooms

Sometimes, all we want are vegetables. Any combination will do, but one of our favorite combinations is carrots, eggplant and mushrooms. All from our local farmers market, of course. It's an easy and delicious combination.

Ingredients

2 large eggplant or 4-5 Japanese eggplant

5-6 fresh carrots

10 shitake mushrooms, washed and de-stemmed

4-5 tbs olive oil

garlic salt

pepper

Instructions

1. Julienne all of the vegetables into thin strips.

2. Heat a bit of olive oil and cook the carrots until they are almost tender.

3. Then combine the eggplant and a bit more olive oil.

4. When the eggplant is beginning to cook and saturated with the oil, place the mushrooms in the pan.

5. Add garlic salt and pepper to taste and continue cooking until all the vegetables are soft.

Broiled Brussels Sprouts

Here's another one of those delicious foods I learned to make when I married my husband. This is so easy – and a big crowd pleaser. Even for someone who doesn't like Brussels Sprouts – these are hard to turn down!

Ingredients

1 bag of fresh Brussels Sprouts (about a pound)

½ cup olive oil

Sea salt to taste

Instructions

1. Turn the broiler on in your oven.

2. Place clean Brussels Sprouts on a cookie sheet and cover them with the olive oil and sea salt.

3. Broil until the sprouts are black.

NOTE: Try the same thing with broccoli. Delicious.

Shaved Brussels Sprouts with Chestnuts

This is a great fall or winter accompaniment, and doesn't take much time.

Ingredients

1 lb Brussels Sprouts

½ lb roasted chestnuts

2 shallots, minced

2 tbs butter

Salt and pepper to taste.

Instructions

1. Wash the Brussels Sprouts and put them through the slicing blade in the food processor.

2. Melt butter in a large skillet, add the shallots, Brussels Sprouts, and chestnuts.

3. Cook just until the sprouts begin to wilt.

DESSERTS

Zabaglione with Fruit

This is a traditional Italian preparation that is a sophisticated dessert. We think this should always be served with a good sparkling wine.

Ingredients

5 eggs, separated

1/3 cup sugar

1/3 cup sparkling wine

1 cup heavy cream

1 tsp lemon zest

Fresh berries

Instructions

1. Place the yolks from five eggs into the top of a double boiler.

2. Add 1/3 cup of sugar and whisk until creamy over steaming water (do NOT let the water touch the bottom of the top pan.

3. When the mixture is creamy add 1/3 cup of sparkling wine and continue to whisk (don't stop!) until the mixture triples in volume.

4. Refrigerate or place mixture over ice to cool.

5. Whip 1 cup of heavy cream until it holds peaks. Add 1 tsp of lemon zest.

6. Fold whipped cream into cooled egg mixture.

7. Spoon over fresh fruit and serve.

Peaches with Fresh Basil

This is an easy and delicious way to serve fresh peaches. We discovered this when we accidently substituted fresh basil for fresh mint. Our guest was the first to discover our mistake, with a huge compliment on our courage to combine basil with peaches. What a happy accident!

Ingredients

6-8 fresh, ripe peaches

6-8 leaves of fresh basil

1/4 cup sugar

Instructions

1. Peel the peaches and remove the pit.

2. Slice the peaches into wedges about 1/8 to 1/4 of an inch.

3. Sprinkle with sugar.

4. Tear (do not cut) the basil leaves into small pieces and add to the peaches.

5. Chill.

Serve alone or with a dip of any good vanilla ice cream.

Pie Crust—For 2 Crust Pie

The secret to good pie crust is to keep the shortening as cold as possible and to chill the dough for at least 30 minutes before rolling it out. OR, if you are scared of pie crust (a family member once commented that our crust was just like his mother's…tough) try a package of Jiffy pie crust mix or one of the prepared crusts. BUT, for those (like us) who keep trying, here is a good recipe.

Ingredients

2 cups flour

½ tsp salt

Pinch of sugar

3-4 tablespoons of butter plus enough shorting to equal 1 cup

3-4 tbs ice water (or more if needed)

Instructions

1. Cut the butter and shortening into the flour, salt and sugar until it is the size of small peas. (Use a pastry cutter or pulse in a food processor.)

2. Add water and mix just until the dough holds together.

3. Chill for at least 30 minutes.

4. Roll out and continue to prepare favorite pie.

Juju's Lemon Tart

I love these. My mother-in-law perfected this recipe, and now each time she asks what she can bring for dinner, I always respond: lemon tarts!

Ingredients

2 cups sugar

1 tbsp cornmeal

1 tbsp flour

4 eggs, unbeaten

¼ cup melted butter

¼ cup milk

¼ cup lemon juice

4 tbsp grated lemon rind

Instructions

1. Mix sugar, corn meal and flour together.

2. In a separate bowl, mix eggs, melted butter, lemon juice and lemon rind together.

3. Add egg mixture to flour mixture.

4. Blend well and add milk.

5. Pour into 12 to 14 medium sized tart shells – or use the pie crust recipe above.

6. Bake at 375 degrees for 12 minutes then 325 degrees for 10 minutes.

Pear Pie

Pears make a yummy alternative to apples in this pie.

Ingredients

6 or 7 pears, cored and sliced in half

½ cup sugar

1 tsp lemon zest

3 tbs fresh lemon juice

1 9-inch unbaked pastry shell

Topping

½ cup flour

½ cup sugar

½ tsp ground ginger

½ tsp ground cinnamon

½ tsp ground nutmeg

1/3 cup butter

Instructions

1. Toss the pears with ½ cup sugar, lemon zest and fresh lemon juice.

2. Arrange them in the unbaked pastry shell. Combine the flour, sugar, ginger, cinnamon and nutmeg and cut in butter until the mixture is crumbly.

3. Sprinkle this over pears and bake at 400 degrees for 45 minutes.

4. We serve this with either whipped cream flavored with a bit of vanilla or almond extract, or with vanilla ice cream.

About the Authors

Larry Burton is from the South: southern Indiana to be exact. He learned to cook by watching his grandmother on the family farm and has never stopped trying new combinations of flavors. Having spent his career as an academic in Boston and Chicago, Larry and his wife, Mary Kay, moved to Little Rock to be near Annamary and their grandchildren. Larry still cooks every day, as well as teaching at the University of Arkansas at Little Rock and at the University of Arkansas for Medical Sciences. He also makes a weekly trip to Argenta for the Certified Arkansas Farmer's Market (rain or shine, cold or hot). One of his greatest joys is serving breakfast to homeless men and women every week. This southern boy has definitely come home.

Annamary Thompson grew up in Boston in a food loving family. Larry is her father, and he never used a recipe (to her knowledge). She then attended college and law school in Illinois and embarked on a life of litigation. Having had quite enough of that, thank you, Annamary began her lifestyle media publication, *Hot in Little Rock*, in 2007. Since then, she and her husband, Greg, have opened a world-class art gallery in the Argenta Arts District in North Little Rock and her business is flourishing. She lives in Little Rock with her husband and children.

LaVergne, TN USA
09 April 2010
178756LV00002B/1/P